CHILDREN IN COLONIAL
AMERICA

by Lydia Bjornlund

FOCUS
READERS

www.focusreaders.com

Focus Readers is distributed by North Star Editions:
sales@northstareditions.com | 888-417-0195

Produced for Focus Readers by Red Line Editorial.

Content Consultant: Bruce Daniels, Professor Emeritus of History, The University of Texas at San Antonio

Photographs ©: Currier & Ives/Library of Congress, cover, 1; North Wind Picture Archives, 4–5, 9, 10–11, 12, 15, 16–17, 18, 21, 24–25, 29, 30–31, 33, 35, 36–37, 39, 41, 42–43, 44; Red Line Editorial, 7; Jim Vallee/Shutterstock Images, 23

ISBN
978-1-63517-874-6 (hardcover)
978-1-63517-975-0 (paperback)
978-1-64185-178-7 (ebook pdf)
978-1-64185-077-3 (hosted ebook)

Library of Congress Control Number: 2018931678

Printed in the United States of America
Mankato, MN
May, 2018

ABOUT THE AUTHOR

Lydia Bjornlund is the author of more than two dozen books for children and young adults. She holds a master of education degree from Harvard University and a bachelor of arts degree from Williams College. She lives in Northern Virginia with her husband, two children, and two cats.

TABLE OF CONTENTS

CHAPTER 1

GROWING UP IN A NEW WORLD

In September 1620, a small, wooden ship called the *Mayflower* set off from England with 102 people on board. Among them were more than 30 children. After 66 days of storms and seasickness, the *Mayflower* finally reached North America. The travelers, also known as **Pilgrims**, landed in what later became the state of Massachusetts. They named their settlement Plymouth, after the town they had left in England.

Rough waves caused one *Mayflower* traveler to fall overboard during a storm.

Nearly half of the people who traveled on the *Mayflower* died during the first winter. Children helped their families survive by gathering wood and berries, fetching water, and tending to the sick. They also helped cook and clean.

The Pilgrims were not alone in the New World. They encountered American Indians whose tribes had lived on the land for more than 10,000 years. As the settlers took over more land, conflict arose between the two groups, often ending in violence.

For the next 150 years, more Europeans settled in the American **colonies**. Many white colonists brought enslaved black people from Africa. The children of enslaved people were also forced into slavery. By 1770, more than two million people lived in Great Britain's American colonies. These included the New England Colonies, the Middle Colonies, and the Southern Colonies.

Throughout the years, children played a key role in the growth of the colonies. Their children, and their children's children, would become the future generations of America.

BRITISH COLONIES IN THE EARLY 1770s ◄

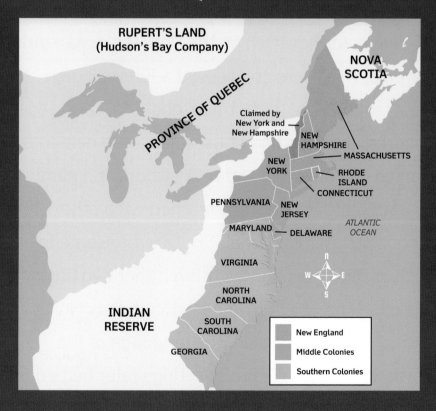

RUPERT'S LAND
(Hudson's Bay Company)

NOVA SCOTIA

PROVINCE OF QUEBEC

Claimed by New York and New Hampshire

NEW HAMPSHIRE

MASSACHUSETTS

NEW YORK

RHODE ISLAND

CONNECTICUT

PENNSYLVANIA

NEW JERSEY

MARYLAND

DELAWARE

ATLANTIC OCEAN

VIRGINIA

N
W   E
S

NORTH CAROLINA

INDIAN RESERVE

SOUTH CAROLINA

GEORGIA

New England
Middle Colonies
Southern Colonies

POCAHONTAS

In 1607, English explorer John Smith arrived at Jamestown, a British colony in Virginia. A few months later, American Indians from the Powhatan nation kidnapped Smith. While imprisoned, Smith met Pocahontas, Chief Powhatan's daughter.

When Pocahontas met Smith, she was only 11 years old. However, by the time Powhatan girls were 13, they were considered adults. Women were responsible for farming, cooking, caring for children, and building houses. Children helped the women by collecting water, firewood, and plants.

Smith and Pocahontas learned each other's languages. In his journal, Smith wrote sentences such as "Bid Pocahontas bring hither two little baskets" and "I will give her white beads" in English and Algonquian, the language of the Powhatan nation. Smith's writings later helped historians learn more about American Indian life.

In 1616, Pocahontas met King James I on her visit to England.

After Smith was freed, colonists in Jamestown suffered a harsh winter. Chief Powhatan sent food to help them survive. Pocahontas often came along to deliver the food. According to some historians, Pocahontas served as a sign of peace between the Powhatans and the colonists.

John Smith. *The Complete Works of Captain John Smith (1580–1631)*. Ed. Philip L. Barbour. Chapel Hill, NC: The University of North Carolina Press, 1986. Print. 139.

CHAPTER 2

SCHOOLCHILDREN OF NEW ENGLAND

Some of the earliest American colonies were settled by Puritans. The Puritans were church-going people who practiced Christianity. In the 1600s, many Christians thought children were born with an evil spirit inside of them. The Puritans formed schools so children could learn to read and study the Bible. The schools also taught children about **morals**. Instructors hoped to teach children how to control their worst instincts.

Similar to most colonial buildings, schools were built primarily of wood.

▲ Some colonial children had to walk or ride several miles to get to school.

In the New England colonies, early laws required towns with a certain number of families to build a school. In most towns, the school consisted of one room and one teacher. This teacher was responsible for teaching children of all ages. Educating all children was a new and unusual idea. In the 1600s, public education did not exist in England. Soon, the Puritans had the highest English literacy rates in the world.

Because many families had farms, New England schools operated around the **harvest** schedule. In the spring, summer, and fall, students were expected to help out on their family's farm. In the winter months, they attended school. Schools often required students to bring a log for the fire, which was the only source of warmth.

Teachers and students had few tools to use in school. Children spent most of their time sitting and reading. One of the earliest schoolbooks was *The New England Primer.* This book was designed to teach children about Puritan beliefs. Students also used a tool called a hornbook. This was a plank of wood with a piece of paper attached to it. A transparent layer of animal horn protected the paper so that children would not get it dirty.

The hornbook usually included the alphabet and a prayer. Students learned their letters by tracing them on the hornbook.

Discipline was important in New England schools. Well-behaved students did not speak unless asked a question. When the teacher entered the room, students stood up from their seats as a sign of respect. Teachers punished bad behavior by hitting students with a whipping rod or making them stand in a corner. If students struggled to learn a lesson, they had to wear a hat known as a dunce cap.

School was different for boys and girls. Most girls in New England went to school only until they learned to read. Parents often wanted their daughters at home to help care for the family. Boys, however, tended to stay in school longer and study advanced topics such as math and Latin.

▲ The dunce cap (far right) was a tall, pointed hat used to punish and embarrass slow learners.

Because of the Puritans' emphasis on education, schooling was more common in New England than in other colonies. For instance, the Southern Colonies had little public funding to create schools. Sometimes, wealthy families sent their sons away to attend school. However, the only education girls received was at home. Many colonial populations received no schooling at all.

CHAPTER 3

ON THE FARM

Early settlers depended on crops for food. For this reason, the majority of colonial Americans lived on farms. American Indians taught the colonists many new farming practices. One of the new crops colonists planted was maize, or corn. Corn was a hearty crop that grew well in the rocky soil of New England. It grew even better in the more fertile soil of the Middle Colonies. Soon, corn became a staple of the colonial diet.

A colonial family divides their last bit of corn among themselves.

▲ A colonial girl brings in her family's cattle at the end of the day.

By the 1730s, farms in the Middle Colonies grew a wide variety of crops. The warm weather and good soil helped plants to grow. These colonies soon grew food to trade with other colonies.

Living on a farm required long hours of hard work. The average colonial family was large compared to families today, consisting of at least six or seven children. And every one of those children was expected to work.

Children who lived on farms woke up as soon as the sun began to rise. After a quick breakfast, they headed off to the fields. In the spring, children helped plant seeds. Older boys loosened the soil by pushing a plow. Younger siblings followed behind, dropping seeds into the soil. In the fall, the entire family worked together to pick crops. On larger farms, families had to make hay to feed livestock such as sheep, cows, and goats.

Children also had daily chores. The youngest children fed chickens, collected eggs, and picked worms off of crops. By the time boys were seven years old, they were responsible for milking cows, feeding the animals, and cleaning out the barn. They also learned to hunt so the family would have meat to eat.

Meanwhile, girls often did chores inside the house. The youngest daughters' chores often included sweeping out the farmhouse. A typical farming family lived in a one- or two-room wooden house with dirt floors. Sweeping out the house helped keep dust away.

As girls grew older, they helped make their family's clothes. Girls typically began using a **spinning wheel** at the age of six or seven. After the boys sheared the sheep, the girls spun the wool into yarn and thread. They also learned to knit and sew. Girls used these skills to make blankets, clothing, and other items.

In addition to sewing, girls prepared and cooked meals. For example, many girls used a butter churn to make cream into butter. Daughters also helped their mothers **preserve** fruits and vegetables so the food would last through the

▲ A young colonial girl helps her mother prepare dinner by peeling apples.

winter. In most farmhouses, cooking was done in a kettle over an open hearth. Girls also used the kettle to make soap and candles from tallow, or animal fat. This was an important task because candles were most farms' only source of light after the sun went down.

MARY JEMISON

In 1753, 15-year-old Mary Jemison was living along Marsh Creek in what is now the state of Pennsylvania. One day, a group of Shawnee American Indians broke into Mary's home and kidnapped her and her family. Although the rest of her family was killed, Mary was not. The Shawnee men gave her to a family of Seneca American Indians, who treated her as if she were their own child.

Mary lived among the Seneca for many years. When she was older, she told her story to a minister, who then published it as a book. "I was very fortunate in falling into their hands," Mary told the minister, "for they were kind, good-natured women." Mary explained that the Seneca were "very tender and gentle toward me."

Much of what historians know about the life of American Indians in colonial America comes

A statue of Mary Jemison stands at her grave in Letchworth State Park in New York.

from stories such as Mary's. Similar to colonial children, American Indian children had many chores to do. However, Mary said the work was not a burden. "Our labor was not severe," she explained. "In the summer season, we planted, tended, and harvested our corn . . . but had no master to oversee or drive us, so that we could work as leisurely as we pleased."

James Everett Seaver. *Life of Mary Jemison: Deh-he-wä-mis*. New York and Auburn, NY: Miller, Orton & Mulligan, 1856. Print. 63, 69–70.

CHAPTER 4

WORKING TO LIVE

In the 1600s, the first settlements in Virginia and Massachusetts drew thousands of people from England to North America. Colonists often used all their money to pay for the journey. Many who could not afford the trip traveled to New England as **indentured servants**. These individuals promised to work for a set period, often seven years, in exchange for their passage. Employers in the colonies covered their fares.

Many indentured servants found work in tobacco fields.

The average age of an indentured servant was 15, though some were as young as 6. Some indentured servants were orphans. Others left behind families in Europe. Their parents had sent them to the New World, hoping they would find more opportunities than at home. The young indentured servants made their new homes throughout the colonies.

The Southern Colonies were in particular need of labor. By the late 1600s, plantations in these colonies were **exporting** tobacco, grains, and other **cash crops**. Farm owners needed many people to care for and harvest the crops. Soon,

> **THINK ABOUT IT**
>
> Why do you think colonists in New England paid for the passage of indentured servants?

plantation owners replaced indentured servants with enslaved people. Slave ships arrived, bringing tens of thousands of people who had been kidnapped from their homes in Africa.

Many enslaved people worked on plantations in the Southern Colonies. Tobacco planters usually relied on slave labor to plant and harvest the crop.

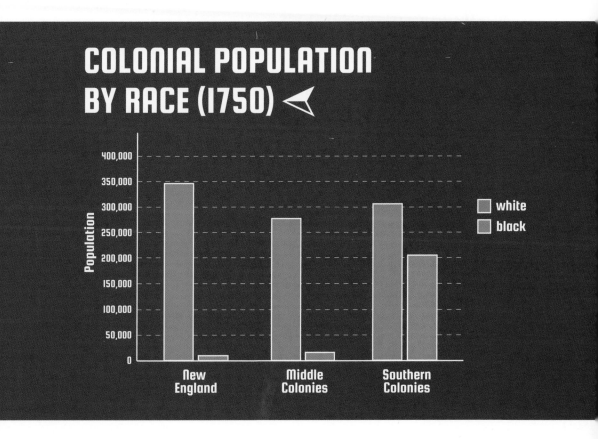

COLONIAL POPULATION BY RACE (1750)

Some hired additional paid workers, but this could be expensive. Many small planters had only one or two enslaved workers. However, some larger plantations depended on the labor of more than 100 enslaved people. On large plantations, enslaved families usually shared cramped huts separate from the main house. They had little to no furniture or possessions.

Enslaved children were forced to do whatever work the plantation owners told them to do. Even very young children worked long hours, often without rest. Children as young as two or three would carry out trash, collect firewood, or fetch water. Some helped the adults in the fields, picking worms off plants or pulling weeds. Plantation owners generally expected children to put in a full day of work in the fields by the time they were 8 or 10 years old. And some

⬆ Some enslaved children worked in slaveholders' homes.

slaveholders tried to make children work harder
by beating or whipping them.

Many enslaved children and their parents lived
in fear of being separated. Slaveholders had the
power to buy or sell slaves at any time. Often, they
would sell the enslaved children as soon as they
were able to work.

CHAPTER 5

JOINING A TRADE

In many colonial families, parents expected their children to learn a trade, or career. Often, families passed down their trades from one generation to another. The first step in learning a trade was completing an apprenticeship. In this agreement, a young person signed a legal contract with a tradesman. By signing the contract, the child agreed to work for the tradesman in exchange for learning the trade.

Many apprentices had to work with dangerous tools such as saws.

Apprenticeships existed in nearly all types of work. Colonial bricklayers, **blacksmiths**, shoemakers, carpenters, and gunsmiths all learned their trades through apprenticeships. Although the majority of apprentices were boys, girls could complete apprenticeships to learn spinning, weaving, or other household work.

In exchange for learning the trade, apprentices had to work hard. In the summer, an apprentice worked as many as 16 hours per day. Apprentices ran errands and performed a variety of odd jobs, depending on the trade. At blacksmith shops, apprentices kept the fire going and gathered the master's tools. Because of their contracts, apprentices had to obey their masters. They even had to receive permission to leave the master's property. The apprentice was not free until the apprenticeship had ended.

▲ A young boy learns from an experienced woodworker.

The age of apprenticeship varied. Many boys began their apprenticeship at six to eight years of age. Orphans and children from poor families often became apprentices at an even younger age.

The terms of apprenticeships also varied greatly. Some apprenticeships lasted for a set period, such as four or seven years. Others ended when the apprentice turned 21 years old.

Young people often became apprentices because their parents could not support them. They needed a way to make their own money. Parents hoped that apprenticeships would provide their child with a better future.

In some cases, town leaders sent children away from their homes to work as apprentices. For example, in New England, church leaders could send children away if their parents had not raised them in the ways of the church. Town leaders could also send children away if their parents had not taught them to read and write.

In some apprenticeships, parents paid a fee to the tradesman. For instance, before becoming a

▲ Benjamin Franklin (right) went on to run his own printing press.

Founding Father of the United States, Benjamin Franklin was an apprentice to his older brother James. Their parents paid James to teach Benjamin the printing trade and to provide him with food and shelter.

CHAPTER 6

CHILDREN AT PLAY

Throughout colonial America, chores, work, and school left little time for children to play. Even so, children managed to find time for fun and games. And because families often had several children, siblings almost always had someone to play with.

Types of play varied greatly from one colony to another. In the strict Puritan villages, adults typically frowned on games. Toys were also rare.

Colonial children played outdoors and cared for pets after finishing their chores.

Instead, families often gave children a young calf or plot of land to care for so they would learn responsibility. In the Middle Colonies, parents' views on play were less strict. Toys of all kinds were more common.

The popularity of toys and games grew during the 150 years of colonial America. As time went on and life became easier in the colonies, both adults and children found more time for play.

Many types of play were meant to help children build life skills. For example, many colonial girls played with dolls. Parents thought dolls would prepare their daughters to someday care for babies. Although very wealthy families could buy porcelain dolls from Europe, most of the dolls in colonial America were made from corn husks or scraps of cloth. Some children used a dried apple for the doll's head.

▲ Children from wealthy families learned to dance at a young age.

Children made other kinds of toys as well. For instance, they used wood and string to make spinning tops and whirligigs. Children also used fishing line as jump rope and string to play cat's cradle. Hopscotch was a popular game because it required only pebbles.

In colonial Williamsburg, Virginia, children played a popular game called rolling the hoop.

To play, children took the rings off of storage barrels. They then used a stick to push the large hoops in a race to the finish line.

Some colonial games are still played today. Children played leapfrog, tag, and hide-and-seek. They also had sack races and relay races. Other common games included ninepin, also known as lawn bowling, as well as ring toss and horseshoes.

Other activities that are popular today were not as common in colonial America. For example, although many colonial towns had been built along rivers, few children knew how to swim. Swimming was considered unhealthy or a waste

➤ THINK ABOUT IT

Play during colonial America differed among regions and families' levels of wealth. Why do you think this was the case? Do you think this is still true today?

▲ Two siblings play together as their family relaxes at the end of a long day.

of time. With the exception of checkers and chess, board games were also fairly uncommon in early colonial America. Instead, children and adults played cards. Cards were fun and inexpensive. In some colonies, children also played games such as tic-tac-toe on the dirt floors of farmhouses.

CHAPTER 7

A CHANGING VIEW OF CHILDHOOD

In the 1600s, people expected children to work just as hard as adults. In fact, many historians say the colony of Plymouth may not have survived without the hard work of children. But by the time of the American Revolutionary War (1775–1783), views of children had started to change. Many adults no longer considered children to be bad or evil. Now, they thought children were **innocent**. They viewed play as a natural part of childhood.

Colonial children played more often as views around childhood changed.

▲ A young girl says goodbye to her father as he goes off to war.

Adults also focused on guiding children toward good behavior instead of breaking their bad habits.

The Revolutionary War significantly affected the lives of colonial children. As children's fathers went to fight in the war, children took on more responsibilities at home. Some boys joined the troops, often as drummer boys. These boys played their drums to instruct soldiers in camp and on the battlefield. The drummers' beats told soldiers when to rise and sleep, turn right or left, and load and fire their muskets. Nearly all of the drummer boys were younger than 16.

Following the Revolutionary War, childhood continued to evolve. As the United States grew, families began traveling west across North America to settle on the **frontier**. Similar to the earliest Pilgrims, these settlers depended partly on their children for survival.

THINK ABOUT IT ◁

How did ideas of childhood in colonial America differ from how you view childhood? How are they similar?

FOCUS ON
CHILDREN IN COLONIAL AMERICA

Write your answers on a separate piece of paper.

1. Write a paragraph that summarizes the main ideas of Chapter 5.

2. If you lived in colonial America, would you rather be an apprentice in a city or a worker on a farm? Why?

3. Which of the following colonial regions was known for its good soil?

   A. Southern Colonies
   B. Middle Colonies
   C. New England Colonies

4. Why did plantation owners rely on slave labor?

   A. Enslaved families were in need of work.
   B. Buying slaves cost less than hiring paid workers.
   C. Paid workers were hard to find.

Answer key on page 48.

GLOSSARY

blacksmiths
Workers who form objects from iron and steel.

cash crops
Plants grown for sale rather than for personal use.

colonies
Areas controlled by a country that is far away.

exporting
Sending goods to other countries or places for sale.

frontier
An area at the edge of a settled or developed territory or country.

harvest
The time of year when crops are ready to pick.

indentured servants
Workers who are bound by contract to work for an employer for a certain amount of time.

innocent
Free from guilt, blameless.

morals
Understanding of good and bad behavior.

pilgrims
People who travel to a place for religious reasons.

preserve
To treat food to prevent it from going bad.

spinning wheel
A machine that uses a turning wheel to make thread from fibers.

TO LEARN MORE

BOOKS

Gilman, Sarah. *The First Thanksgiving.* New York: Enslow Publishing, 2016.

Miller, Brandon Marie. *Women of Colonial America: 13 Stories of Courage and Survival in the New World.* Chicago: Chicago Review Press, 2016.

Pratt, Mary K. *A Timeline History of the Thirteen Colonies.* Minneapolis: Lerner Publications, 2014.

NOTE TO EDUCATORS

Visit **www.focusreaders.com** to find lesson plans, activities, links, and other resources related to this title.

INDEX

Answer Key: 1. Answers will vary; **2.** Answers will vary; **3.** B; **4.** B